MW00881785

Mountain Mill Editorial

We love hearing feedback from our readers. If you have the chance to leave us a review, we would greatly appreciate it. Your feedback on Amazon is vital to us.

Follow this QR Code to find our books on Amazon:

Follow us on Instagram: @mountainmilleditorial

Authors

Liudmyla Pytel & Javier Montero

Content

SWITZERLAND. KRAMPUS

In Swiss folklore, while Santa Klaus rewards good children with gifts, his obscure counterpart, Krampus, punishes mischievous ones.

Krampus is often depicted as a horned anthropomorphic figure who roams the streets during the holiday season, scaring children and carrying away particularly mischievous ones in his sack.

Santa Klaus and Larissa

In the heart of Switzerland's high mountains and deep valleys, a story is told that has been passed down from generation to generation, for centuries.

Santa Claus, the jolly old man in a red suit and beard as white as Alpine snow, was said to have a daunting job every Christmas. He spent his days and nights reading letters written with the innocent hope of children all over the world, and his hands did not stop preparing the toys that were requested.

In his huge, candlelit study, Santa kept an old, worn-out book. On it were the names of the children who had been especially good during the year. Larisa, a pure-hearted girl who lived in a little house in the mountains, was on that list. But when Santa read his letter, he was met with an unusual request.

Larisa didn't want dolls or trains; His wish was that his brother would give up his antics and stop being a constant headache for the town.

Santa knew he had to create something extraordinary for Larisa's brother, but he also wanted to give her a gift she could enjoy on Christmas morning.

That's when Santa thought of Krampus, the creature whose name made many children cringe. Krampus, born in Alpine mythology, and known for his terrifying horns and thick fur, was said to take away animals and frighten villagers with his antics.

With his plan in mind, Santa bundled up and stepped out into the cold of the night, riding his reindeer-drawn sleigh, and setting off in search of Krampus. It wasn't hard to find him, as Krampus was doing his thing on a farm.

Upon presenting himself to Krampus, Santa asked for his help in teaching a lesson to the naughty children, especially Larissa's brother. Krampus, at first surprised by Santa's visit, soon became thrilled at the idea of scaring the children into improving their behavior.

–Fantastic! What a great idea! Do I kidnap them in a sack along with the chickens? The demon asked excitedly.

"No, no, Krampus, we mustn't overdo it either. I'm just asking for a lesson... Look, on Christmas night, I'll leave gifts for the children who have behaved well. The idea is that you come in and leave them something they can't play with so that this serves as a warning to them...

"And what do I leave them?" A stone? The bones of my chickens?

"How about coal?" Santa Claus said then.

–Charcoal! And they'll get their hands dirty! Fantastic! But you really don't want me to take one in my bag? Then I would give them back...

"No, no, Krampus, that's too much. We'll settle for coal.

"All right, deal done. Just seeing the look of disappointment on their faces... Hahaha! - And the demon licked his lips with pleasure at the thought that he could do some evil, even if it seemed very mild to him.

That Christmas, as you can imagine, Larisa received a mountain of toys, while her brother, unwrapping his gift, found nothing but a large lump of coal along with a note that read: "If you improve your attitude, and stop misbehaving with others, next year you will receive the same gifts as your sister".

And so, a new tradition was born. Children who have behaved well throughout the year are given toys, while disobedient children find a lump of coal in their socks.

FRANCE. PÈRE NOËL AND THE RÉVEILLON

Père Noël is the French Santa Claus. Children leave their shoes by the fireplace on Christmas Eve, and Père Noël showers them with presents. La Réveillon is a very late festive dinner held after Midnight Mass on Christmas Eve.

Élise Wish

In a small town in the north of France, where it's always cold in winter, the houses twinkle with lights that resemble stars. Everyone awaits Père Noël, the man who brings gifts and joy. La Réveillon, the night before Christmas, is especially magical. Families gather for a feast, and children fight sleep to catch a glimpse of Père Noël with his presents.

In a quaint house by the forest's edge, there lived a girl named Élise, who felt the village's collective anticipation but harbored a personal wish. She didn't yearn for toys or sweets; Élise longed for La Réveillon to be shared with her father, who worked in the distant city and seldom made it home.

Élise's mother, a woman of warm gaze and skilled hands, had prepared their home for Père Noël's visit with care. The dishes for La Réveillon were set succulent oysters, a golden roast turkey, and the sweet scent of bûche de Noël wafting from the oven. Yet, the empty chair by the hearth stood as a silent testament to the absence of Élise's father.

"Do you think Père Noël could bring Dad home tonight?" Élise asked, her voice a blend of hope and skepticism.

"Père Noël can do many things, but some are beyond even his reach," her mother responded softly, her own heart echoing the wish.

As night fell, bringing La Réveillon with it, the village was enveloped in a symphony of laughter and carols. Élise, eyes fixed on the window, watched the snow descend in quiet flurries, cloaking the world in hushed white.

Time passed, and Élise's eyelids drooped, her spirit sinking slightly. She nestled into the couch, the fireplace's glow warming her cheeks as she drifted into slumber.

At midnight, as Christmas officially began, a gentle knock on the door sliced through the stillness. Élise, startled by the sound, rushed to open it, half-expecting to see Père Noël in his grand red coat. Yet, instead of the jolly old fellow, stood a tall, weary man, holding a suitcase in one hand and a present in the other. It was her father, with a smile that outshone the night's brightest stars.

"How...?" Élise gasped, disbelieving.

"Tonight, even the most unlikely wishes can come true," her father said, embracing her tightly.

Elise's mother, hearing the commotion, rushed to the door, and joined in the embrace. La Réveillon was complete, and Père Noël's magic had worked in a way that neither Élise nor her mother could have imagined.

They sat together, savoring every moment, sharing stories, and laughing. There were gifts, of course, but none as precious as the family reunited. As the snow continued to fall outside, a sweet sense of gratitude filled the house, evident in every laugh and every meaningful look exchanged.

Père Noël, from somewhere in the snowy night, gave a knowing wink before vanishing into the darkness, aware that his work in that little house by the woods was more than fulfilled. La Réveillon had delivered its own miracle, and the magic of Christmas had once again been revealed.

GREECE. KALLIKANTZAROI

These are goblin-like creatures that emerge from the earth during the 12 days of Christmas to cause mischief. Greek households can keep them away by burning logs during those days.

Fig Cake and Kallikantzaroi

In a hidden corner of Greece, there is a small village near the mountains and the sea. The village grandparents tell a story about the Kallikantzaroi, mischievous elves that they only visit during the twelve days of Christmas. They say that on those days, magical things can happen if you blow a wish into the wind.

The Kallikantzaroi were known for their love of mischief and their disdain for sunlight, living underground the rest of the year, working tirelessly to see the World Tree, the one that holds the Earth and keeps it from collapsing into the abyss. But during those twelve days, their work ceased, and they came to the surface to dance under the starry mantle and play pranks on the unsuspecting villagers.

It was a time when mothers warned their children to play late outside and elders murmured protective incantations about their homes. But there was one boy, named Nikolas, whose curiosity was as great as the Aegean Sea. Nikolas had heard of the Kallikantzaroi

since he was a child and longed to see these creatures from his childhood tales.

The night of the winter solstice, when the shadows stretched farther than at any other time and the world held its breath at the renewal of the solar cycle, Nikolas ventured into the forest. She carried with her a piece of fig cake that her grandmother had made and a small flashlight.

He entered the labyrinth of ancient trees until he reached a clearing, where legend had it that the Kallikantzaroi would appear. Hidden behind a laurel bush, Nikolas waited nervously for the creatures to appear.

It wasn't long before the air was filled with thunderous laughter and the sounds of messy footsteps. The Kallikantzaroi had arrived, clumsy and playful, their eyes glowing with a red light and their teeth like coal chips. They danced and jumped, creating a whirlpool of chaos that made dead leaves rise like frightened birds.

Nikolas, overcoming his initial fear, came out of hiding and approached them. At first, the Kallikantzaroi stopped, as surprised to see a human as he was to see them. But Nikolas offered his cake and with a smile, he held out his hand in peace.

The dark beings sniffed the air, attracted by the scent of the candy. Cautiously, one of them walked over and took the cake, tasting it with an expression of astonishment that soon turned to delight. What followed was an evening of shared laughter and unusual dances, with Nikolas learning the strange steps of the Kallikantzaroi.

At dawn, the creatures bid Nikolas farewell, giving him a small charcoal tooth as a souvenir. They warned him to return home before the sun rose and to keep their meeting a secret.

Nikolas ran back to the village, coal tooth clenched in his hand and a story he could never fully tell. Every year, on the longest night, I would leave a piece of cake in the forest clearing, and every morning, it would have disappeared, replaced by a small mark on the ground: a dance footprint of the Kallikantzaroi.

Thus, forged an unusual friendship, between a child and the creatures of the shadows, a reminder that even in the most ancient traditions, there is room for understanding and wonder, and that magic sometimes lies in the simple courage of an open heart.

SWEDEN. GNOME TOMTE

In Sweden, there is an enchanting Christmas tradition that involves a magical creature called Tomte, a gnome from Scandinavian folklore who plays the role of Santa's helper. He is known for being the guardian of the farms and taking care of the animals and the people who live on them.

On Christmas Eve, as Santa Claus prepares to deliver gifts to children around the world, it is said that the Tomte visits homes to leave gifts and sweets for children, placing them in the shoes they leave in the window. He is a beloved and respected figure who brings joy and protection to homes, and although he is shy and avoids being seen, his generous and caring spirit is felt by all.

The tradition of Tomte is so beloved in Sweden, that many families leave it a bowl of buttered porridge on Christmas Eve as a thank you for its help and to ensure that their homes continue to be blessed by its magic for the year to come.

The Legend of Tomte, Santa's Shy Helper

A Swedish legend tells that long ago, Tomte, a Scandinavian gnome, met Santa Claus and became his diligent helper. But how did it happen and what were its motives?

Tomte was a tiny, agile being, known for his kindness and cheerfulness. Although capable of mischief if someone mistreated others or animals, his true passion was to bring joy to others. However, he was so shy that he always avoided being seen by humans.

One cold winter's night, on Christmas Eve, Tomte saw a flashing red light among the trees. Upon investigating, he discovered a reindeer with a shiny nose and a trapped leg. Next to the reindeer was a man with white beard and red clothes: it was Santa Claus.

"Ho, ho, ho," Santa Claus exclaimed when he saw the little being. A tiny goblin!

"I'm a gnome, not a goblin," Tomte corrected gently.

"Excuse me, a gnome. "What's your name?" asked the old traveler.

"Tomte," said the gnome.

"Well, Tomte, I'm Santa Claus. I need to free my reindeer Rudolph to deliver gifts to the children. Could you lend me a hand? - Santa asked.

The gnome, delighted with the idea of giving gifts to children, helped Santa Claus and then they shared a hot chocolate in his humble abode. During the talk, Santa Claus saw in Tomte the perfect companion for his Christmas task.

"Would you like to be my helper in the delivery of gifts?" It's a task I do every December 24th," Santa Claus proposed.

The thought of seeing the children's happiness was enough to convince Tomte.

"Of course!" the gnome agreed.

That same night, Tomte accompanied Santa Claus, watching him hand out the presents.

"Santa Claus," Tomte said later, "I'll help you every year, but I'll go in through the door, not through the chimney." I'm so small that I'll go unnoticed.

"Ho, ho, ho..." Of course, Tomte, as you prefer," Santa Claus replied with a smile.

Since then, Tomte has been Santa's helper, bringing gifts to Scandinavian children every Christmas. Although they try to catch a glimpse of him, the cunning gnome is never seen, perpetuating the mystery and magic of Christmas.

BASQUE COUNTRY. OLENTZERO

Olentzero is a traditional figure of Basque Christmas. According to legend, he is a charcoal burner who comes down from the mountains on Christmas Eve to bring gifts to children. He is usually depicted as a robust man wearing Basque farmer's attire, wearing a beret, smoking a pipe, and sometimes with a glass of wine or cider in his hand.

Today, like other European Christmas traditions, children write letters to Olentzero asking for gifts. The cities and towns of the Basque Country celebrate their arrival with parades. On Christmas Eve, children sing Olentzero carols, and sometimes a man dressed as Olentzero joins in the festivities.

Olentzero, The Charcoal Burner of the Basque Mountains

I n a forest in the Basque Country, surrounded by pine trees and mountains, the legend of Olentzero originated. It tells the story of a boy who was found alone in the woods, with a curious, lively look that stood out in the darkness of the night, and his only companion was the sound of branches snapping under his bare feet.

On a moonless night, the fairies of the forest, moved by the child's purity and sadness, decided to take care of Olentzero. Using their songs and their magic, they bestowed upon him extraordinary strength and a big heart, capable of deeply feeling and loving many.

Olentzero grew up among the creatures of the forest, learning the silent language of nature and the art of turning wood into charcoal, black as moonless nights, but warm as the hugs he never had. He became a charcoal burner, and his life was spent between the crackling flames and the isolation of his cabin in the high mountains.

But everything changed on a cold winter's night. As the stars embroidered constellations of stories on the

An unusual light captured Olentzero's attention. A star, brighter and more beautiful than any other, danced among its heavenly sisters. With his curiosity stoked by the fairy magic still beating in his veins, Olentzero knew that the glow signaled something extraordinary.

Leaving behind his home and his solitude, he set out on a journey that would take him beyond the borders of his beloved forest, through valleys and rivers, until he reached the promised lands of Bethlehem. There, in the humblest place, he saw the child who would change the world, the baby Jesus. And though Olentzero had no riches or treasures to offer, he gave the most humble and heartfelt gift: a toy carved with his own hands hardened by work.

That's when Olentzero understood his true purpose. He returned to the Basque Country, but he no longer did it alone. Every Christmas, with his sack full of toys carved with love and dedication, he toured the towns and villages, leaving gifts in the homes of the children, filling their hearts with joy, and perpetuating the magic that once saved him.

Every year, Olentzero's story is reflected in the children's smiles, their hopeful eyes, and the simple

gifts they lovingly give. This charcoal burner, favored by fairies, is now a symbol of Christmas in the Basque Country, proving that what matters most is not material gifts, but feelings that come from the heart.

PORTUGAL. CONSODA

On Christmas morning, the Portuguese have a tradition of putting extra places at the breakfast table for deceased relatives. This is believed to ensure good fortune for the household.

The Breakfast of Souls in Consoda

I n a small village in northern Portugal, where the hills are dressed in green even in winter and the air smells of eucalyptus and firewood, Inés' family kept alive an ancient tradition, as woven into the thread of their history as the patterns on their wool blankets. It was the tradition of the Consoda, the Christmas breakfast, where not only the living was fed but also those who were no longer with us were honored.

Ana, barely eight years old, had learned from her grandmother the importance of remembering. "They are like the roots of an olive tree," her grandmother would say, her hands always moving, kneading bread, or cradling the air as if caressing the heads of those she could no longer touch. "Invisible under the earth but keeping the tree alive."

That Christmas, Anne felt the excitement bubbling in her chest like water in a clay pot over the fire. It was the first time he had been allowed to help put the extra seats on the table for deceased relatives. Under her mother's gentle gaze and grandmother's proud supervision, she carefully spread out the tablecloth embroidered with silver threads, placing the plates, wine glasses, and cutlery reverently, as if they were offerings.

With the first ray of light slipping through the window and dispersing into the liquid gold of the oil

on the plates, the family gathered around the table. The empty chairs were not a reminder of loss, but of the ethereal presence of those they had loved and lost. The aroma of roasted cod mingled with the sweet perfume of freshly baked bread, flavored with anise and orange.

"Ana," her mother whispered, "you can begin."

With trembling hands, Anne lifted the jug of wine and poured some into each of the empty glasses, her heart beating to the beat of an ancient drum, the echo of those who came before. He closed his eyes and recited the poem he had learned, a song of welcome to the souls who visited them in spirit:

"Come, dear ones of the past,

Join us in this day of feasting,

Our home is your home,

Our hearts, your endless refuge."

When she opened her eyes, she saw the chair of her grandfather, who had died when she was still very young, and it seemed to her that she could see the outline of his figure, a trembling in the air like heat on flames.

Breakfast was filled with laughter and memories, stories of past childhoods and forgotten adventures that came to life on the lips of the family. Each member shared a memory, a ribbon they wove around the table, uniting the living with the dead in a warm embrace.

At the end of the meal, Ana noticed how her mother placed a piece of bread on the empty plates, a gesture that transcended time and space. And as the shadows played at the foot of the olive trees and the sun rose, lifting the morning mists, Anne understood the gift of tradition.

It was not just an act of remembering, but an act of celebrating continuity, the certainty that love and memory were the true breaths of immortality. In that Consoda, Anne not only gave thanks for the harvest and the family, but for the eternity they found together at the Christmas breakfast table.

NORWAY. THEY HIDE BROOMS

In a small village surrounded by snow-capped mountains and lush forests in Norway, there is an ancient and peculiar tradition on Christmas Eve. It was said that, at midnight, witches roamed free, looking for brooms in houses to soar through the night sky and perform their dark magic.

That's why Norwegian families hide all the brooms in the house to prevent them from being stolen by witches and evil spirits on Christmas Eve.

The Mysterious Coins of Christmas Eve

O nce upon a time there was a very curious boy named Lars. She grew up hearing her elders' stories about Christmas Eve witches, and although she hoped to catch one every year, she had never seen one. That Christmas Eve, he decided it would be different.

"I'm going to find out if witches are real," he told himself with a mixture of fear and excitement.

While his family adorned the house and hung lights and garlands, Lars set his plan in motion. Instead of hiding his broom, he carefully left it behind the front door, hidden but accessible.

"If the witches come, I'll surprise them!" she thought.

Night came and with it a silence covered the town. Lars, lying on his bed, pretended to sleep, but kept a half-lidded eye, attentive to any noise. The minutes passed slowly, and the anticipation was mixed with fear.

Suddenly, a faint crack broke the silence. Lars, his heart pounding, saw a shadow creeping through the moonlit window. "It's them!" he thought. Stealthily, he climbed

out of his bed and peered into the living room, where the shadow was now dancing strangely.

With a jump, Lars turned on the light and was shocked to discover not a witch, but her cat, Nils, playing with a small toy broom that had been forgotten next to the Christmas tree. Lars let out a nervous laugh.

After that incident, as Lars placed the toy broom out of Nils' reach, he noticed something unusual: on the floor lay a small shiny object. It was an ancient coin with inscriptions I had never seen. Had she been left behind by a wandering spirit, or had she simply fallen out of some forgotten bag?

The boy decided to believe in the first option, feeling that he had touched a corner of the mystery surrounding Christmas Eve. From that year on, Lars always left a broom in the same spot, and every Christmas Eve he would find a new old coin on the floor.

Over the years, Lars grew and coin collecting became the subject of many stories he told his children and grandchildren. And while many in the village wondered if the Christmas Eve witches were anything more than a fairy tale, for Lars, they would always be a sign of the magic and mysteries that live in the traditions of his home in Norway.

PHILIPPINES. GIANT LANTERN FESTIVAL

In the city of San Fernando, the "Giant Lantern Festival" is held every December, where huge and elaborate lanterns are displayed and compete to be the most beautiful.

The light of San Fernando

I n a small town in the Philippines, known for the affection of its inhabitants and the beauty of its sunsets, a story of light, hope and creativity is told.

The story begins with little Matthew, a boy with skilled hands and a heart full of dreams.

Every year, as the December breeze began to blow, Mateo watched with shining eyes as the "Giant Lantern Festival" kicked off in San Fernando.

His family, of humble means, could not afford to buy the materials to build one of those magical lanterns that lit up the night like stars fallen from the sky. But Mateo had something more valuable than money: an overflowing imagination and the desire to create.

With pieces of paper, bamboo sticks that he collected on his walks in the countryside and the help of his grandfather, he began to build his own lantern. It wasn't big or ostentatious like the ones competing at the festival, but every piece was glued together with love, every thread stretched with hope.

As the lantern took shape, neighbors began to gather around Mateo's house, marveling at the boy's passion and talent. Mateo's grandmother, with hands that wove light like fabric, taught him how to create patterns that told stories of ancient warriors and mysterious seas.

The night before the festival, Mateo finished his work, although small, Mateo's lantern was a tapestry of colors that reflected the history of his people, their legends, and their dreams.

With everyone's help, they placed their lantern in the center of the village, not to compete, but to share. As the lights came on and the giant lanterns began to spin, Matthew's lantern shone a different light.

It wasn't the biggest, or the most complex, but its light was warm and inviting, and people stopped not just to admire it, but to feel a part of it.

That year, the "Giant Lantern Festival" would be remembered not for the competition, but for the lantern that brought a community together.

Matthew and his lantern became the living reminder that true beauty is born in the simplicity and unity of a people.

ICELAND. JOLABOKAFLOD

Jólabókaflóð, in Icelandic, which translates to "Book Flood" in English, is an Icelandic holiday tradition. It involves the exchange of books as gifts on Christmas Eve and then spending the evening reading them. The tradition is very popular in Iceland and stems from a time when imported paper was one of the few things not rationed during World War II. As a result, books became the gift of choice, as they were one of the few items that could be easily transported and given during the holiday season.

The Night of the Paper Whispers

I n the heart of Reykjavík, where Christmas lights flicker like fireflies in the winter cold, the Ólafsson family cultivated a tradition as warm as their home in the warmth of the fireplace. In Iceland, Christmas Eve brought with it a tide of stories and knowledge: the Jólabókaflóð, the flood of Christmas books.

The Ólafsson house, with its spacious living room and wooden shelves full of volumes of all sizes, was the perfect setting for this tradition. Elin, the mother, had spent weeks searching for the perfect book for each member of the family, carefully wrapping each volume in shiny paper and tying them together with a gold bow. The children, Sigur and Lisa, held back the excitement of knowing that they would soon have a new world at their feet, a fresh adventure between their fingers.

Christmas Eve arrived and with it, after a dinner where traditional Icelandic flavors were mixed with laughter and sharing, the most awaited gifts were delivered. At the foot of the tree, by the glow of the fire, a pile of books was waiting to be discovered.

Sigur received a collection of Norse sagas, adventures of heroes and gods that fueled his love of history and mythology. Lisa, with shining eyes, opened a picture book of fairy tales, her imagination.

ready to soar through the magical landscapes and deeds of brave princesses.

Jón, the father, held a book of poetry in his hands, the whisper of verses ready to transport him to worlds of beauty and contemplation, while Elin opened a novel of intrigue and mystery, a story that would keep her awake until the early hours of the morning.

The family settled into their living room, wrapped in blankets and with steaming hot chocolates in their cups. As the winter wind whistled outside and the snow began to fall, the Ólafssons immersed themselves in the silent concert of turning pages and murmurs of excitement.

It was a night in which they shared not only gifts but experiences, laughter, and whispers about stories that led them to sail tumultuous seas and fight with winged dragons. On this night of books, time stood still, and the outside world vanished, leaving only the glow of

candles, the melody of pages, and the indestructible bond of a family united by the love of stories.

As the night crept into the early hours of Christmas, the children's eyes slowly closed, but their dreams were filled with the adventures they had begun to read. And in that house, every Christmas Eve, the Jolabokaflod brought with it a flood of memories.

and traditions that would live forever in the hearts of the Ólafssons.

TURKEY. ST. NICHOLAS AND THE HANGING SHOCKS

The Turkish tradition regarding St. Nicholas and hanging socks originates from the story of Bishop Nicholas of Myra, a historical figure who lived in ancient Lycia, a region that is now part of Turkey. According to legend, St. Nicholas, known for his generosity and compassion, learned of an impoverished family with three daughters who could not marry for lack of dowry. To help them anonymously, Nicholas threw bags of gold down the chimney of their home. The bags fell into the socks that the girls had hung up to dry in the heat of the fire. The next day, they found the coins and were able to marry, thanks to the kind intervention of St. Nicholas. Since then, the tradition of hanging socks in the hope of receiving gifts has become a symbol of generosity and the spirit of giving in the holiday season.

St. Nicholas' socks

A beautiful Turkish legend tells that a long, long time ago, a single father and his three daughters lived in a simple abode in the valleys of Lycia.

The man had lost his wife and worked tirelessly, but he could not accumulate enough money to offer a dowry for his daughters for when they wished to marry.

The family's economic situation was so precarious that the young women only owned one pair of winter boots each, so worn that every time they went out, they returned with socks soaked by snow.

One day on Christmas Eve, the daughters returned home crying. They stripped off their boots and spread out their socks by the fire, waiting for them to dry. Their father, grieving, asked them the reason for their sadness...

"Father," said the eldest, "I am deeply in love with a brave soldier, but our love is impossible without a dowry.

"And I," said the second, "have fallen in love with the village master, but I am in the same misery as my sister."

"It's the same with me," added the youngest, "I'd like to marry my beloved, the musician, but without a dowry, it's an unattainable dream..."

The father, devastated by the helplessness of not being able to help his daughters, joined in his tears:

"Forgive me, my dears, for not having the means to assure you of a happy future.

That same night, however, the kindly Bishop Nicholas, who would later be known as Santa Claus, was passing by and heard the whole conversation through the half-open window. Moved by compassion and his generous heart, he decided to sneak into the house that night to leave them a present.

The bishop did not wish to be discovered, so he slipped down the extinguished chimney. Noticing the hanging socks, he filled them to the brim with gold coins.

At dawn on Christmas Day, the sisters discovered the gold in their socks and their joy was immense: they now had what they needed to be able to get married!

Moved by the happiness he had brought to the young women, Nicholas decided that, henceforth, every Christmas Eve he would bring gifts to the most disadvantaged families.

Thus, was born the beautiful tradition of hanging socks for Santa Claus to deposit his Christmas presents.

MEXICO. THE CHRISTMAS FLOWER

The Euphorbia Pulcherrima plant is native to tropical regions of Mexico. Commonly known as Christmas Flower, Christmas Eve, Pastora, Pascuero, Poinsettia, Federal Star or Poinsettia in the USA.

The flowers are shaped like the star of Bethlehem and their vibrant red color symbolizes the blood of Christ. Legend has made these flowers a must-have in Christmas decorations around the world.

The Legend of Esmeralda and Christmas Eve

In a secluded town in Mexico, surrounded by hills that rise to the sky, there was a little girl named Esmeralda. He had a big and generous heart, although his family didn't have many resources.

Like every year, the arrival of Christmas Eve brought with it a procession of faith and gratitude. The villagers made their way to the church with gifts in hand to offer to the Infant Jesus. Esmeralda, however, was empty-handed and heavy-hearted. Poverty robbed her of the opportunity to share a physical gift, but she couldn't bear the thought of walking down the aisle with nothing to offer.

As he walked down the lonely path, tears welled up in his eyes, moistening the earth in his wake. It was then that a whisper, as faint as the touch of a feather, touched his ear. Esmeralda looked up, and before her stood an angel, whose light was the promise of dawn.

"Emerald," said the angel, "the true offering is born from the heart. Choose something from the earth, something that everyone has overlooked, and with love, make it your gift."

Looking around, Esmeralda saw only weeds, plants without flowers or fruit that the other villagers despised. With trembling hands, he picked up a bundle and carried it with him. Upon entering the

church, he went to the altar and, with his eyes closed, deposited his humble offering.

The temple was filled with whispers and curious looks. Esmeralda opened her eyes and, together with the villagers, witnessed the miracle: where once there were only green branches, now red stars were bursting, as vivid and bright as if they had captured a fragment of the night sky.

A murmur of astonishment swept through the church. The weeds had transformed into poinsettias, with petals that seemed to embrace every hope and every dream.

Since that miraculous Christmas Eve, the flower has become an emblem of hope in the small village. And every year, at the turn of the season, the villagers remembered the story of Esmeralda, the girl who, with a pure heart and the blessing of an angel, transformed the ordinary into the extraordinary, teaching everyone that the humblest of gifts can hold the greatest of wonders.

GREENLAND. SANTA'S REINDEER

The tradition of Santa's reindeer has its roots in Norse poetry and mythology, but was popularized by Clement Clarke Moore's 1823 poem, "A Visit from St. Nicholas," also known as "The Night Before Christmas." In this poem the original eight reindeer are named for the first time: Dasher, Dancer, Prancer, Vixen, Comet, Cupid, Donner, and Blitzen.

The story goes that these magical reindeer have the unique ability to fly, and every Christmas Eve, guided by Rudolph the Red-Nosed Reindeer, a later addition to the legend, they carry Santa Claus in their sleigh full of toys. They leap from rooftop to rooftop, delivering gifts to children around the world in a single night, driven by the spirit of generosity and goodwill.

The Magical Christmas Reindeer Caravan

On the eve of the most magical night of the year, as the stars twinkle and snow covers the land, a special caravan prepares for an epic journey. These are not common reindeer; they are the magical reindeer that carry with them the essence of the Christmas spirit, allowing Santa Claus to spread hope and joy in the form of gifts during Christmas Eve.

In charge of these reindeer are the diligent elves, magical beings who, with their deft hands, make sure that each reindeer is ready and in top shape for the great journey. Not only do these goblins take care of the reindeer, but they also infuse them with energy and magic, allowing them to fly through the starry skies.

Guiding this flying sleigh, we find nine legendary reindeer, each with their own unique personality and talent:

Donner: Known as the Thunder, with a powerful and bold spirit.

Blitzen: Lightning fasts as lightning and lights the way on the darkest nights.

Vixen: The Playful, always with mischief up his sleeve, adds fun to the ride.

Cupid: the lover, who with his tenderness, spreads love wherever he goes.

Dazzling and brilliant, the Comet leaves behind a trail of stardust.

Dasher: The Fiery, with his inexhaustible energy, propels the group forward.

Dancer: The Dancer, with his graceful movements, dances among the clouds.

Prancer: the Acrobat, who jumps and glides gracefully in the air.

But, at the head of them all, with his distinctive, bright red nose, is Rudolph, the guide, the beacon that lights the way in the darkest night. Although he was the last to join this mystical caravan, his bravery and kindness made him the natural leader.

As they fly, the reindeer line up in a special order: on the left, the male reindeer, and on the right, the females, with Rudolph bravely leading the way. Together, they cross mountains, seas, and cities, bringing the magic of Christmas with them to every corner of the world.

GERMANY. THE FIR TREE

The tradition of the Christmas tree began in Germany in the 16th century. Martin Luther is believed to have been one of the first to adorn a tree with candles, mimicking the stars in the night sky for his family. Over time, this custom spread throughout Europe and then America. Fir trees, with their evergreen leaves, symbolize eternal life and are decorated with lights and ornaments during Christmas, culminating in a star or angel at the top representing the Star of Bethlehem or the announcement of the birth of Jesus. Today, the Christmas tree is a focal point of celebrations and family gatherings.

The Legend of the Fir Tree, Guardian of Christmas

Years ago, on a cold and silent night, the city of Bethlehem witnessed a miracle: a child, destined to change the world, was born in a humble corner. The stars shone brighter, and the angels descended to sing praises and announce his coming.

From all corners, people of all lineages and social classes came, bringing gifts to honor the heavenly child. Next to this sacred place, three trees erected their trunks: an elegant palm tree, a hundred-year-old olive tree, and a young fir tree.

The palm tree, with its majestic height, exclaimed:

"I will offer one of my most beautiful palms to the divine child. May it protect you and give you warmth on this cold night.

The olive tree, with its wisdom, said:

"My olives will be a balm for your skin, giving it radiance and softness like angels."

The fir tree, feeling small and without gifts to offer, questioned in a trembling voice:

"What could I, a mere fir tree, offer the son of God?"

"Your pointy blades might hurt him!" replied to the palm tree haughtily.

"And your resin could soil their garments," the olive tree added condescendingly.

The fir tree, with a heavy heart, whispered:

"It's true, I don't have any gifts worth offering..."

However, an angel, who had witnessed everything from the shadows, saw the sincerity in the heart of the fir tree. As night fell, he summoned the smallest and brightest stars and asked them to adorn the branches of the fir tree. In an instant, the fir tree lit up, surpassing in beauty any other tree.

The little Jesus, waking from a peaceful sleep, laid his eyes on the shining fir tree and smiled with purity and joy.

From that magical moment, the humble fir tree was elevated to be the symbol of Christmas. Today, in every corner of the world, she adorns herself with love and hope, remembering that day when having nothing material to offer, she conquered the heart of the divine with her sincere humility.

ITALY. LA BEFANA

Like Santa Claus in style, but very different in appearance, the Befana is a witch who has become a big part of Christmas celebrations in Italy. The most popular version of the story is that she was a kind woman who gave food and shelter to the three Wise Men as they were on their way to visit the baby Jesus.

She is presented as an old witch who rides a broomstick, and who usually wears a black shawl and carries a goodie bag. She is supposed not to like to be seen and is said to beat any child who spies on her. A smart way to keep the kids in bed while the parents organize the gifts.

The Legend of La Befana, the Star Seeker

In a village hidden among the hills of Italy lived La Befana, a wise and solitary old woman, known for her gifts of herbalism and her deep knowledge of the sky and the stars. Their home always smelled of fresh herbs and freshly baked bread, and their door was always open to anyone in need of advice or comfort.

One cold winter's night, while La Befana was stargazing, three majestic figures approached her abode. They were the Three Wise Men, who, guided by a singularly bright star, were looking for the newborn Jesus to pay homage to. Knowing the purpose of their journey, they invited La Befana to join them in their sacred mission.

However, preoccupied with her chores and tired by the passing of the years, La Befana declined the offer, wishing them a safe journey and offering them shelter for the night. But while the Kings slept, a feeling of uneasiness invaded the old woman's heart. Had he made the right decision?

The next morning, seeing that the Three Wise Men had already resumed their journey, La Befana, full of

remorse and with the ardent desire to see the Child Jesus, packed some gifts and mounted on her broom.

Jesus packed some gifts and rode on his

broomstick, following the star that shone on the horizon.

Although she searched tirelessly, she was never able to find the Christ Child. However, her generous spirit led her to leave gifts in the homes of the children she met on her way, hoping that one of them would be the little Savior.

Since then, every year, on the Eve of the Epiphany, La Befana flies over Italy, leaving gifts for good children and coal for those who have been naughty. He continues to search for the Child Jesus, and although he has not found him, his habit of giving gifts is still alive, teaching us that what is important is not always what we seek, but the act of seeking itself.

DENMARK. JULEKATTEN

Known as "Julekatten", this monstrous cat is said to roam the snowy countryside during Christmas. The cat eats anyone who hasn't been given new clothes to wear for Christmas. This tale likely originated as an incentive for farmers to finish their fall work in time for the festive season.

Tobias and Julekatten

In a small village nestled in the Nordic mountains, where the nights are long and the legends as old as the rustling of snow under the boots of the villagers, there lived a boy named Tobias. He was known in the village for his boundless imagination, which often led him to daydream while tasks were half-done, scattered like leaves in autumn.

Tobias, with his wheat-colored hair and eyes as clear as the winter sky, had a particular aversion to chores. "Later," he used to say, but that after rarely came. His mother often reminded him of the consequences of laziness, especially as Christmas approached. In the cold lands of Denmark, it wasn't Santa Claus who worried about children's antics or laziness, but a much more mysterious and ancient being: Julekatten, the Christmas Cat.

Legend had it that Julekatten was a huge, magical cat that patrolled the snowy countryside, peering through its eyes bright like shooting stars, looking for children who hadn't finished their annual labors. To the workers he left gifts and blessings, but to the idlers, only the echo of his own repentance.

As Christmas approached, fear gripped Tobias' heart. She had promised to knit a new sock to hang on the fireplace, but the sock was still just a ball of wool, and her other tasks were just as incomplete. His mother, with a sigh, told him, "Tobias, every stitch you don't take, every task you leave unfinished brings you closer to Julekatten's stealthy steps."

On Christmas Eve, as the full moon peeked out of Tobias' window, a subtle noise woke him up. It was a low, resounding purr that filled the room with ancient vibrations. Tobias knew, without a doubt, that Julekatten had come looking for him.

He got out of bed and, armed with only his bravery, stepped out into the deep, cold snow. There was

Julekatten, majestic and terrifying, his fur dark as the darkest night and his eyes reflecting the full moon. The cat looked at him and, with a soft meow, asked, "Where are your finished tasks, little Tobias?"

Tobias, his voice trembling, confessed his tendency to dream instead of work. Julekatten listened and then, with a wave of his huge head, took Tobias on a magical journey. He showed him how every task accomplished was a thread in the fabric of the world, how every finished task was a star in the firmament of character.

When they returned, Julekatten disappeared as quietly as he had come, leaving behind only a trail of footprints in the snow and a wool that seemed to shine with its own light. Tobias, his heart pounding, and his hands now determined, worked through the night. She wove, cleaned, and tidied up, and by dawn, the sock was ready and hung, the tasks completed, and her heart full of pride.

Julekatten never visited Tobias again, as he was no longer needed. Every Christmas, a new stocking, knitted with care and love, hung from the fireplace, and Tobias' chores were always completed. But in the village, it was whispered that sometimes, on the clearest, coldest nights, a purr of approval could be heard echoing through the mountains, reminding everyone of the importance of responsibilities fulfilled and dreams woven with one's own hands.

AUSTRIA. THE CHRISTMAS WREATH

In Austria, the Christmas wreath, known as "Adventskranz", is an endearing tradition that marks the countdown to Christmas. Usually composed of fir branches and decorated with ribbons and Christmas balls, the wreath has four candles that are lit successively each Sunday of Advent. With each candle that is lit, families gather in a moment of reflection and togetherness, anticipating the arrival of the holiday. This act symbolizes the light and hope that grow with the approach of the birth of Jesus, bringing joy and warmth to the heart of the German winter.

Crown candles

Four candles were burning in the Christmas wreath.

The first candle sighed deeply and said:

"My name is PEACE. I give light to people, but for some reason, people don't want to live in peace."

Its flame grew smaller and smaller, and soon it was completely extinguished.

The second candle flickered rapidly and said:

"My name is FAITH. But no one really needs me. People don't want to know anything about God. And because of that, it doesn't make sense for it to continue to burn here."

Suddenly, there was a draught of air, and the second candle was extinguished.

The third candle spoke softly and sadly.

"My name is LOVE. But I don't have the strength to keep burning anymore. People don't pay attention to me. They only see themselves and don't show any love to others."

And the third candle also went out after it had shone for a moment.

Suddenly, a child rushed into the room. He looked at the extinguished candles and said:

"No, no! They must burn, they cannot be extinguished!" And she began to cry.

However, the fourth candle spoke. Said:

"Calm down, little one! Don't be afraid! As long as I burn, you and I can light the other candles. My name is HOPE."

And so, the boy lit a match with the candle called HOPE and brought his flame to the other three candles. Thus, the four candles began to burn together again.

The End

Made in the USA
Las Vegas, NV
03 December 2023

82009938R00059